Tracks through time

Archaeology and history from the London Overground East London line

Museum of London Archaeology

for

Transport for London

Published in June 2009 by Museum of London Archaeology
© Museum of London 2009

A CIP catalogue record for this book is available from the British Library

ISBN 978-1-901992-87-8

**Written, designed and photographed by
Museum of London Archaeology**

Principal authors: Aaron Birchenough, Emma Dwyer,
Nicholas Elsden and Hana Lewis
Additional text and Editors: Sue Hirst and Susan M Wright
Design and production: Tracy Wellman
Photography and reprographics: Andy Chopping
Illustrations: Carlos Lemos
Project Managers: George Dennis and Nicola Powell

ACKNOWLEDGEMENTS
TfL would like to thank everyone involved in the East London Line Project
Team, and the Balfour Beatty Carillion Joint Venture, who helped facilitate
the archaeological works and standing building recording undertaken by
Museum of London Archaeology, and enabled these works to be completed
in conjunction with the successful implementation of the construction works.

In particular, thanks are due to:

East London Line Project
Peter Richards – Director, London Overground Infrastructure
Leo Carse – Delivery Manager, Infrastructure
Barrie Noble – Construction Manager, Northern Extension
Nick Humby – Project Manager, Phase 1a
Jon Colclough – Environment Manager

BBCJV
Mike Casebourne – BBCJV Project Director
Andy Swift – Section Manager
Garren Reddy – Senior Engineer
Phil Wharton – Line of Route Section Manager
Andy Bradshaw – Construction Engineering Manager

English Heritage
David Divers and Mark Stevenson

Special thanks are also extended to Steve Haynes, from **Arup**, for
assisting in the management of the archaeological and standing
building recording works, and for providing specialist advice to TfL.

IMAGES AND PHOTOGRAPHIC CREDITS
Ashmolean Museum 18, 23
City of London, Metropolitan Archives 37
Devonshire Fine Art 46
Ermine Street Guard 13 (left)
Essex County Council / Roger Massey-Ryan 10 (top)
Essex Record Office 55
Graham Field 27 (bottom)
Guildhall Library, City of London 51 (top & bottom), 56
Hackney Archives 65 (right)
Ian Galt / Museum of London 58
John Sturrock front cover, 6
Mary Evans Picture Library 54
Museum of London 11 (top right), 12, 47 (left), 50
Museum of London / Derek Lucas 10 (bottom), 12 (left)
Museum of Witchcraft 49
National Portrait Gallery, London 29 (top)
National Railway Museum/SSP 57 (centre), 60
Richard Lea / John Schofield 20 (bottom)
Royal Albert Memorial Museum and Art Gallery, Exeter 45 (bottom left)
The Schøyen Collection 20 (top)
TfL from the London Transport Museum collection 52 (all), 53 (right, top &
centre)
Tower Hamlets Local History Library and Archives 61 (centre), 63 (bottom)
The Trustees of the British Museum 36
Weald & Downland Open Air Museum 32

Contents

Foreword 4

Introduction to the East London Line Project 7

Earliest times in Shoreditch 9

Roman London: beyond the city walls 13

From Anglo-Saxon times to the 12th century 17

Holywell Priory 19

The Tudor mansion of the earls of Rutland 27

The Great House and the Stone House 31

Bricks, brickearth and Brick Lane 35

Eastenders – suburban development in the 17th century 39

East London life in the 18th century 43

The origins and construction of the East London line 51

The Great Eastern Railway 55

The impact of the railway on Shoreditch 59

Bishopsgate Goods Yard 61

Life after the railways in Shoreditch 63

The railways arrive in Dalston 65

All change! Dalston today 67

What happens after the excavation? 68

And finally . . . 69

London Overground: the capital's new rail network 70

Places to visit / Further reading 72

Foreword

TfL was delighted to work with Museum of London Archaeology to undertake the archaeological investigations and historic building recording that have been completed along the route for the new London Overground East London line. In doing so, we have gained an insight into London's history.

The new line will run along the route of one of London's earliest railways. When we started the project it was clear that we were working not only in an area of significant historic railways, but also in an area of archaeological importance that would reveal interesting archaeological features and provide information to help in our understanding of the people and communities that have lived along the line for hundreds of years. We were all very excited to hear that Museum of London Archaeology had uncovered parts of the medieval Holywell Priory. Another example of the exciting discoveries that were made was the finding of the witch bottle.

While building this railway on such historic infrastructure has resulted in some engineering challenges for the team here at Transport for London, the work of Museum of London Archaeology has also been welcomed by the people working on the project as it has given us all the opportunity to be involved in protecting the heritage of the area.

We are delighted to present this publication describing the work undertaken and its findings.

Peter Richards
Director, London Overground Infrastructure

The 1960s Holywell viaduct being modified for the new East London line in Shoreditch (looking north)

4

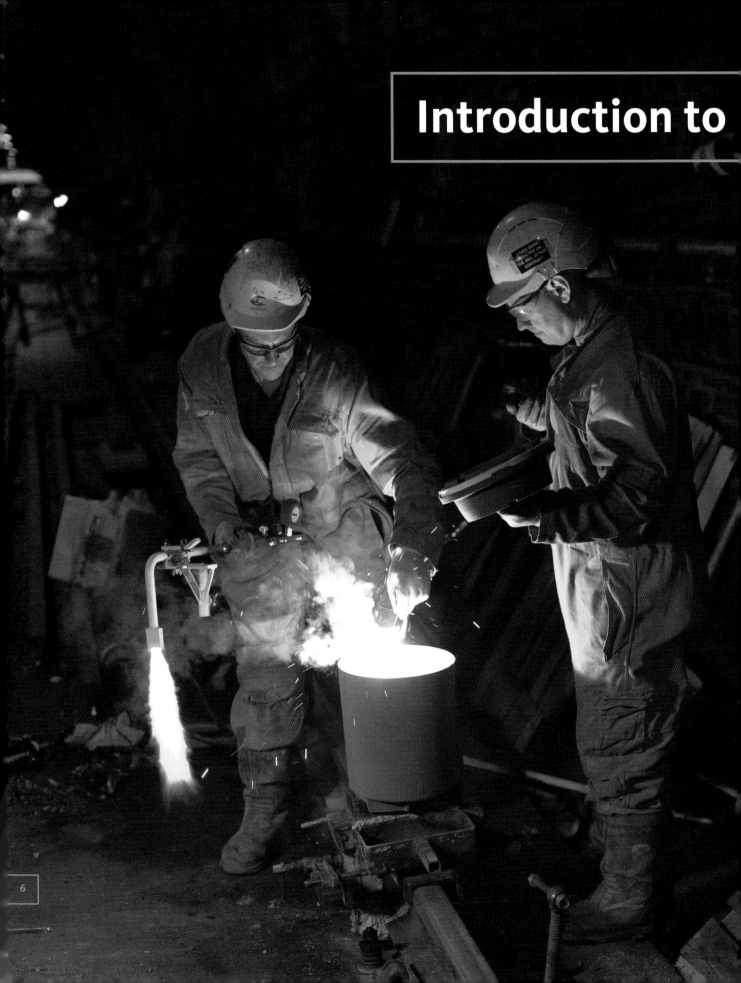

Introduction to

the East London Line Project

The East London Line Project is London's latest urban railway, but it has its roots firmly in history, linking several earlier railways. The project includes upgrading the original East London Railway from Wapping to Shoreditch (1869) which incorporated Marc and Isambard Brunel's pioneering Thames Tunnel (1843).

North of Shoreditch, the new East London line includes a new bridge over the Great Eastern Main Line into Liverpool Street (1874), and a new elevated viaduct and station across the former Bishopsgate Goods Yard (1880). Crossing Shoreditch High Street on another bridge, the viaduct crosses the site of medieval Holywell Priory, before joining an existing viaduct from the former North London Railway, which ran into Broad Street (1865). The North London Railway viaduct is being repaired and upgraded, including major works to the former cuttings and covered way at Dalston (1865), where the new East London line will join the Richmond to Stratford line, forming part of London Overground.

London's newest railway has, therefore, presented a unique opportunity to discover more about some of London's earliest railways, as structures have been demolished and cleared for new construction. This includes previously undiscovered parts of one of the world's first operational passenger railways, the Eastern Counties of 1840. The new construction has also led to the important archaeological discoveries spanning the prehistoric, Roman, medieval, Tudor and later periods, particularly at the site of Holywell Priory and beneath Bishopsgate Goods Yard, described in this book.

Maps showing the location and route of the East London line, with detail showing the Holywell Priory (HLW06) and Bishopsgate Goods Yard (BGX05) sites (hatching shows all areas investigated)

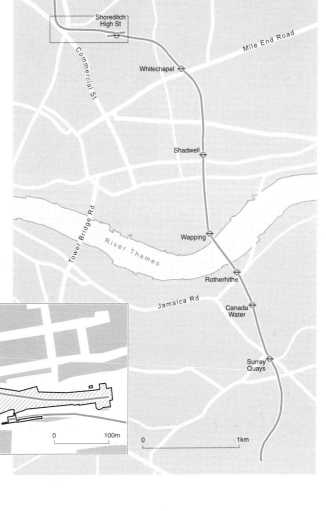

7

Construction workers on the East London line

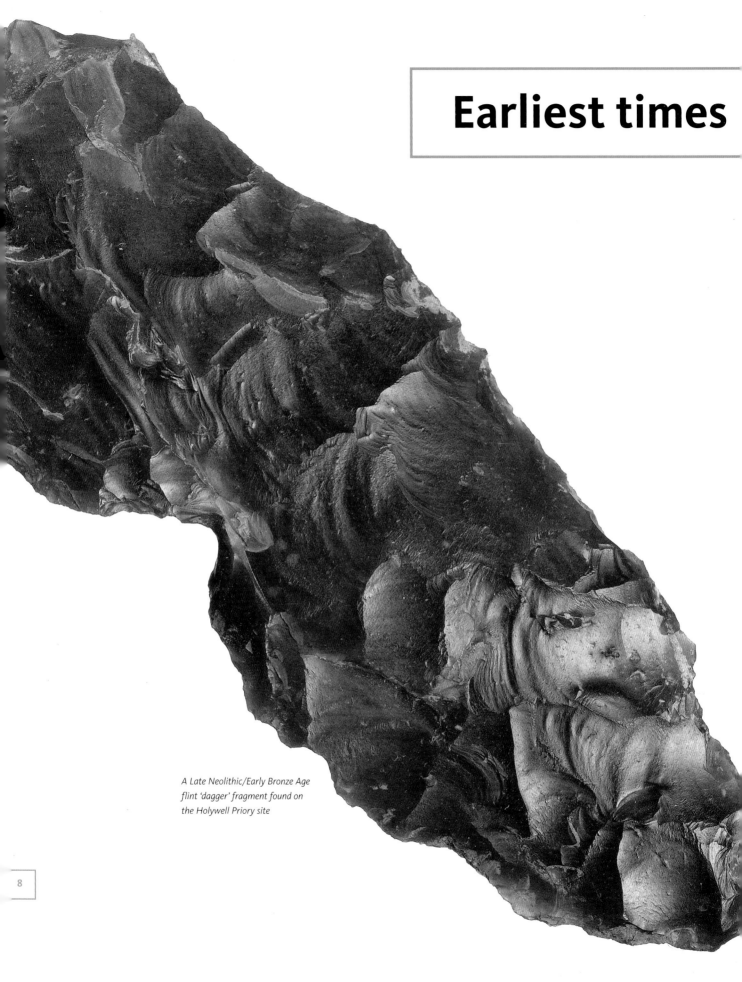

Earliest times

*A Late Neolithic/Early Bronze Age
flint 'dagger' fragment found on
the Holywell Priory site*

A reconstruction of the Walbrook valley (centre right) and the Thames in prehistoric times, before the founding of London

The Thames valley takes the form of a series of steps or terraces carved into the valley sides by the prehistoric river during a series of alternating periods of higher and lower water flow as the landscape froze and thawed, over the last half-million years. The river cut successively deeper, but narrower, channels, producing the stepped terraces. During the periods of lower and slower flow, gravels and sands were laid down by the river across each terrace.

Some terraces are capped with a clay-silt informally known as 'brickearth', for instance in southern Shoreditch where several of the larger excavations took place for the East London Line Project. This combination would later provide well-drained fertile soils that were very suitable for agriculture, and the brickearth, as its name suggests, would provide raw material for construction from the Roman period onwards (see below).

The latest and lowest terrace, the Thames floodplain, was formed at the end of the last Ice Age, some 15,000 to 10,000 years ago, and is covered with alluvium (water-lain silts, clays and peat) deposited as the sea and river levels rose over the following millennia.

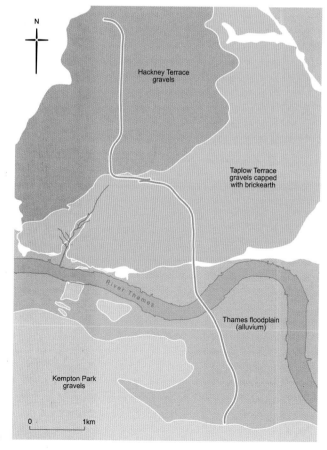

A geological map of prehistoric London showing the present-day course of the Thames and the East London line

In the area of what would become the City of London and Shoreditch, a series of small streams flowed into a larger channel known as the Walbrook, which in turn ran into the Thames. These streams have since been filled in or covered to form sewers or drains, but would have provided convenient water supplies up to at least the medieval period.

The earliest evidence for human activity from the East London Line Project was over 70 pieces of prehistoric struck flint: tools and the waste from making them. The majority were found near a tributary of the Walbrook stream – this water source is likely to have formed a focus for prehistoric activity in the area, from early hunters after animals attracted by the water, to later farmers watering their animals and crops. Not only were tools such as scrapers for preparing animal hides, adzes for woodworking and knives found, but also numerous fragments of waste from flint knapping, showing that tools were being manufactured by the prehistoric inhabitants.

These finds originate from the wandering hunter-gatherer groups of the Mesolithic period (c 10,000–4000 BC) through to the settled farmers of the Bronze Age (c 2500–600 BC), and show that the Shoreditch area has been inhabited for perhaps 10,000 years.

Any other evidence of what these people were doing here has been removed by later activity. However, excavations elsewhere in London would suggest early wandering bands camping for relatively short periods whilst they hunted and foraged for wild foods. By the Bronze Age people had settled in permanent farmsteads, raising animals and growing crops in field systems covering large tracts of the Thames valley.

Reconstruction view of a Late Bronze Age farm based on evidence from Lofts Farm, near Maldon, Essex

Ploughing in the Bronze Age: reconstruction of cultivation based on evidence from Bermondsey

Flint tools

Flint tools are some of the most durable and long-lived artefacts used by man, and are often found where organic materials such as bone and wood have completely decayed. Some of the earliest flint tools in this country date from the Lower Palaeolithic period and were made up to half a million years ago.

Scrapers – as the name suggests scrapers were tools used for scraping. One of their uses would have been the removal of fat and flesh from animal hides as part of the tanning process, as well as for working soft materials such as wood or bone.

Adzes – whilst axes are used to cut wood etc to a rough form, adzes are tools which are used to shape, smooth and sometimes hollow out the item. Examples of this might be the employment of an adze for the timbers of a house, or in the construction of a dug-out canoe.

Knives – are some of the everyday objects that before the introduction of metal *c* 2500 BC were made out of flint.

Knapped flint tools can be as sharp as modern surgical instruments!

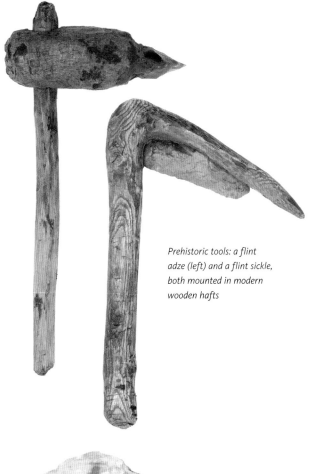

Prehistoric tools: a flint adze (left) and a flint sickle, both mounted in modern wooden hafts

A Mesolithic tranchet adze found on the Bishopsgate Goods Yard site

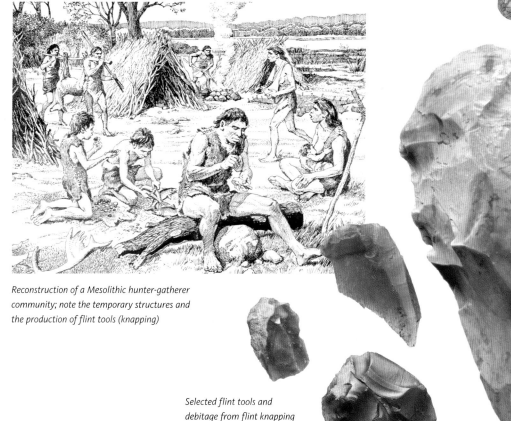

Reconstruction of a Mesolithic hunter-gatherer community; note the temporary structures and the production of flint tools (knapping)

Selected flint tools and debitage from flint knapping found on East London line sites

Roman London:

beyond the city walls (AD 43–c 410)

Britain was annexed by Rome following the invasion under the Emperor Claudius in AD 43. *Londinium* (Roman London) was established within a decade of the Romans' arrival. The Romans built a strong network of roads to move troops and supplies as they pushed the frontier of the Empire further north into Britain. As the new province was pacified, more peaceable trade and communication were also dependent on the road network linking the growing number of towns.

Ermine Street was the main Roman road leading north out of *Londinium* to *Lindum Colonia* (Lincoln) and *Eboracum* (York). 'Ermine Street' is a much later Anglo-Saxon title, and the Roman name for the road is unknown. It left *Londinium* at the later Bishopsgate, one of the seven gates in the city wall, and was constructed between AD 47 and AD 75, being extended at the same rate as the Roman frontier was pushed north.

The Holywell Priory and Bishopsgate Goods Yard sites straddle the probable route of Ermine Street in Shoreditch. However, the only evidence found for the road was a possible roadside ditch on the western side of Shoreditch High Street. It is therefore assumed that in this area the Roman roadway would have lain somewhere beneath the modern road surface.

Ditches and pits indicate rural land management in the Roman period at the Holywell Priory site and, with other finds of Roman pottery, brick, and tile, hint at some level of local occupation in this area some 900m outside the city walls.

1st- or 2nd-century Roman mortarium (a vessel with a gritty surface for grinding foodstuffs eg spices); sherds of similar vessels were found at the Holywell Priory site

View of Roman London in the early 2nd century AD

Members of the modern Roman re-enactment group, the Ermine Street Guard, marching along the road

Burials beside Ermine Street

The most significant Roman find from the project was an isolated group of two burials found at the Holywell Priory site, adjacent to Ermine Street. Roman cemeteries and individual burials were located outside the town limits, and many were placed along roadsides. Part of the extensive northern cemetery of *Londinium* has been found beside Ermine Street at Spitalfields, *c* 300m to the south of these burials. The Holywell burials may be outliers of that cemetery or, perhaps more likely, isolated roadside burials in a predominantly rural area.

At Holywell, two male adults were found in a grave over a silted-up Roman boundary ditch; the third burial, of which only the skull survived, was nearby. The lower of the two skeletons was in a crouched position; no grave goods were found. One of the men had a healed collarbone fracture. This injury suggests he had lived a very tough physical life, probably toiling on the farmland around *Londinium* or driving cattle.

A Roman burial at the Holywell Priory site: two adults were placed in one grave, the lower one in a crouched position and the upper laid supine

Map showing Roman burials around Londinium *and the site of the Holywell burials*

the site

Fleet

Roman city wall

Ermine Street

Walbrook

River Thames

N

0   500m

*Reconstruction view of the late Roman burial of a wealthy woman in
Londinium's northern cemetery at Spitalfields*

From Anglo-Saxon times to

the 12th century (*c* AD 410–1150)

It is believed that the name Shoreditch (like Hoxton and Haggerston) is of Saxon origin, and that a church may have been established there before the Norman Conquest of 1066, probably around what is now St Leonard's church, some 300m to the north of the Holywell Priory site.

The only Saxon finds from the East London Line Project sites were an antler comb fragment, a bone pin and some cooking pot sherds dated to *c* AD 970–1150, found at Holywell. The only feature excavated at Holywell which may have been Saxon in origin was a ditch, filled with rubbish and later medieval pottery. However, radiocarbon dates indicate the ditch could have been dug in the Saxo-Norman period, between AD 990 and 1160. This suggests only a limited human presence in this area around the time of the Norman Conquest. Layers interpreted as alluvial marshland deposits probably represent the open 'moor' which later formed the initial lands of Holywell Priory (see below).

During the late 11th to 12th centuries Shoreditch grew into a village on the old Roman road (modern Shoreditch High Street in this area), probably centred on St Leonard's church, and surrounded by agricultural land and moorland. Rubbish pits containing pottery of this period were found just to the east of modern Shoreditch High Street at Bishopsgate Goods Yard. This suggests some limited occupation, or at least activity, along the road at, or just before, the first documentary reference to Shoreditch in the mid 12th century and the foundation of Holywell Priory.

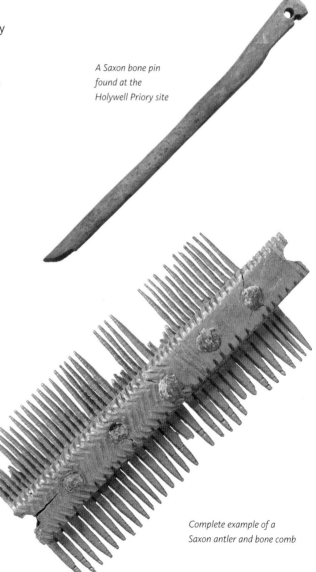

A Saxon bone pin found at the Holywell Priory site

Complete example of a Saxon antler and bone comb

Excavation of medieval pits at Bishopsgate Goods Yard

Holywell

18

Priory

The foundation and growth of the priory

The priory of St John the Baptist at Haliwell, or holy well, was founded in Shoreditch by 1158, probably between 1152 and 1158. Holywell Priory, as it has come to be called, was actually a nunnery, founded for female religious who lived a celibate common life and followed the rule of St Augustine; they are described as Augustinian canonesses. The heyday of Augustinian foundations, for men and for women, was in the 12th century. The first London house was Holy Trinity Priory, for men, founded just inside the city wall at Aldgate in 1107 or 1108 by Queen Matilda.

With its sister houses, St Mary Clerkenwell (founded c 1145) and St Mary Kilburn (founded c 1130), Holywell was one of only 23 houses of Augustinian canonesses in England and Wales, and one of a small group of nunneries in and around London. These included, as well as the Clerkenwell and Kilburn houses, St Helen's Bishopsgate (Benedictine, before 1216) and the Minoresses outside Aldgate (Franciscan, 1293).

The initial grant for the religious house at Holywell came from another religious, this time male. Robert son of Gelran (or Generan), a canon of St Paul's Cathedral, made the grant of the site of the future priory: 3 acres (1.2 hectares) of 'moor' which included the natural spring, the haliwell, on the west side of the high road. These 3 acres with their water supply must have formed the north part of what came to be the nuns' enclosed site or precinct.

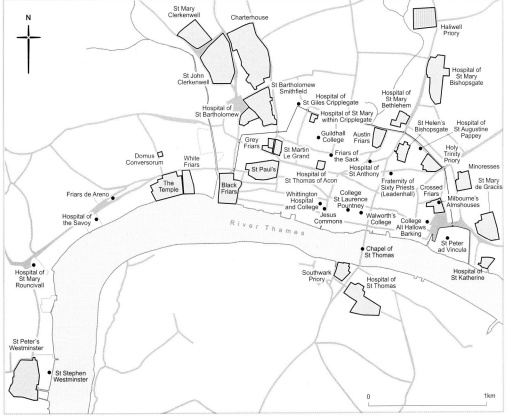

The religious houses of medieval London and its environs

Lead token from c 1270–1350 from Holywell Priory, showing a squatting ape looking in a mirror

Wyngaerde's panorama of London, c 1540; the tower and spire of Holywell Priory can be seen top right

Gifts of more land, from Richard de Belmeis, Bishop of London, and another 3 acres from Walter, precentor of St Paul's, quickly followed and increased the site of the priory to about 8 acres (3.3 hectares). It lay in the north angle between the high road and Holywell Lane which led to Finsbury Fields to the west. The area of the precinct is clearly shown on later maps and measured around 200m by 170m (see eg the Agas map of *c* 1562 and Chassereau's map of 1745, below, pp 27 and 43).

Holywell was a 'suburban' rather than rural nunnery: it was sited outside the city walls and surrounded by fields, but it was on a main route into the city – the former Ermine Street which became Holywell Street and later Shoreditch High Street – and only 900m north of the city gate at Bishopsgate. The main gateway into the priory was on the quieter south side, on Holywell Lane, rather than on the highway.

The priory's landholdings increased rapidly for the next 50 years or so, through gifts from a large number of individuals and by purchase; the nuns' property was spread throughout the south-east, from Cambridgeshire to Kent, and included arable, meadow and pasture land, marsh, mills, rents and churches. From the early 14th century these lands were increasingly leased out for rent. But their most important holdings were in London, in particular, houses and shops. Between the 1250s and the 1350s, a large number of London citizens and their widows left the priory small City properties and rents. After that date London citizens mostly bequeathed sums of money, some of which may have been used to purchase City property. When Holywell's income was assessed in 1535, two-thirds came from rents in London.

Nunneries were in general not as wealthy as religious houses for men, but Holywell, like St Mary Clerkenwell, was one of the richer, with a total net income in the 1530s of about £300. It was still considerably poorer than the neighbouring Augustinian priory for men, Holy Trinity Aldgate, whose London property alone was worth about £355 in 1537. Some 190 nunneries are known in medieval England. Holywell would have been the ninth richest when the priory was closed in 1539 as part of the Dissolution of the monasteries by Henry VIII.

A 'concord' (land transfer agreement) between Roger de Bray, Margery his wife and his son Milo, and the house of Haliwell and Magdalena the prioress, regarding land owned by the priory in Dunton, Bedfordshire; c *late 12th century*

A reconstruction of the interior of the church of the wealthier Augustinian priory of Holy Trinity Aldgate in c *1300, looking east*

The church and precinct

Within the nuns' enclosed precinct were all the buildings necessary for their daily religious and domestic life. A reconstruction of the possible layout of these buildings at the Dissolution was published as long ago as 1920; this is based on the detailed descriptions and measurements in leases of the site of the priory in the 1540s, immediately following its seizure and closure, and subsequently in the following centuries, as the property passed from owner to owner, combined with a large amount of conjecture.

This 1920 reconstruction shows in the north-east quarter of the precinct the nuns' cloister (open courtyard) and chapter house (where they met to discuss business), together with the domestic buildings – their dormitory, refectory and infirmary – and private gardens. The building ranges run northwards from the church. The gardens extend up to the main road, and the nunnery is approached from the south through the gate and gatehouse on Holywell Lane. In the north-west quarter are the stables, dovehouse, barns, granary and other service buildings. Grouped around a great or inner court are the brewhouse, bakehouse and various houses, presumably to accommodate officials, visitors and others. Also shown are two wells, one in the orchard to the north and another in the inner court, just south of the washhouse. The position of the cloister north of the church is one known from other nunneries, including St Mary Clerkenwell.

The plan of the church shown on this reconstruction is wholly conjectural, with the possible exception of the line of the south wall, partly because the church was rapidly demolished at the Dissolution. It shows a large two-part structure. Here there is a south aisle, with on the north side the nuns' choir adjoining their cloister, west of the 'night stairs' which gave them access to their dormitory, with a great choir to the east and a doorway for the priest to the sacristy where the vessels used in the mass were kept. This 'parallel aisle' arrangement is often found where there is a need to separate the nuns from the parishioners when the priory church also serves as the parish church, as at St Mary Clerkenwell and St Helen's Bishopsgate. The priory church of Holywell was not, however, the parish church – there is apparently only one reference to a parish of Holywell.

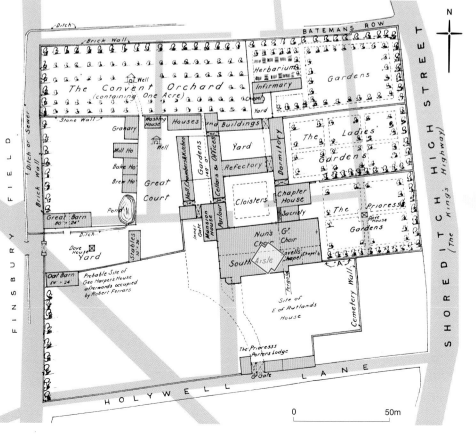

The conjectural plan of Holywell Priory published in 1920 in the Survey of London, *overlaid with the outline (in red) of the excavated area within the church*

Bone rosary beads from the Bishopsgate Goods Yard site

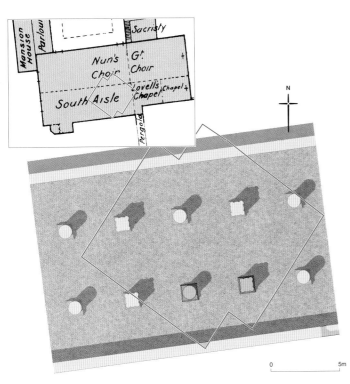

The results of the archaeological excavation indicate that the first stone church on the site was a very different structure. The remains of two lines of piers which would have carried arches were found; these consisted of robbed-out pier foundations on the north, but the lowest courses of two columns and their bases survived on the south; the style of the pier bases indicates a date of *c* 1180–1200. This suggests the late 12th-century church had a central nave separated by arcades from north and south aisles. Both nave and aisles were narrow, *c* 4m and 3m respectively, suggesting the church was cruciform in plan. Finds from the excavation suggest the interior was embellished in the 13th century with decorated tiled floors, and the columns were painted – traces of red and green paint survived.

Plan of the excavated nave and aisles of the 12th-century church compared with (upper) the Survey of London *conjectural plan; the* in situ *piers of the south arcade and remains of the south aisle wall are highlit in dark orange; the excavation area is outlined in red*

The in situ *12th-century quatrefoil pier and square pier base of the south nave arcade*

The in situ *12th-century circular pier and square pier base of the south nave arcade, with part of an* in situ *floor tile bottom right; the base has an unusual corner 'spur' design*

Letter 'A' from a tomb brass from Holywell Priory

In the later medieval period the north arcade piers were demolished and replaced *c* 1m to the north. Widening the church on the north side would have affected the adjacent cloister and ranges, and required a major rebuilding programme. Perhaps the north aisle was not widened and the arcade was replaced for other reasons. The densely packed graves indicate that this area was a popular place for burial in the later period, suggesting a chapel or chapels here. Some rebuilding certainly took place in the early 16th century when Sir Thomas Lovell built himself a chantry chapel, where two priests were to pray for his soul after his death and burial there in 1513. Lovell was a former Speaker of the House of Commons and Treasurer of the king's household. The building work may have been more extensive, affecting other parts of the church: the windows were reglazed with inscriptions exhorting the nuns to pray for Lovell and a gallery was built connecting the chapel with lodgings to the south. This gallery is described in 1544 as covering the south aisle of the church; Lovell's chapel is variously referred to as on the south side of the church or of the choir.

Holywell Priory features on Wyngaerde's panorama of London of *c* 1540, providing a distant view of how the priory may have appeared at the Dissolution. Here the church is indeed a cruciform structure. It is shown with a long narrow nave (left), of probably six or seven bays with tall lancet windows, a central crossing tower with a spire and a two-part east end (right); two buildings project to the south – an aisled south transept and to its east a second building, perhaps the Lovell chapel.

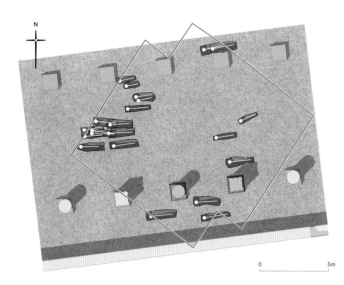

Plan of the excavated nave and aisles of the later medieval church and of the excavated burials – note the widened nave; the in situ *piers of the south arcade and remains of the south aisle wall are highlit in dark orange; the excavation area is outlined in red*

Holywell Priory: detail of Wyngaerde's panorama of London of c *1540*

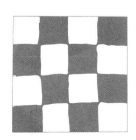

'Westminster'-type tile designs found at Holywell Priory

The community

The religious community was small, governed by a prioress. In 1379 there were 11 nuns who had taken vows, while at the election of the prioress in 1472 seven nuns and ten novices were present. When the priory was closed as part of the Dissolution of the monasteries by Henry VIII in 1539, the prioress, sub-prioress and 12 nuns received pensions. Some nuns were the daughters of London families; many brought lands and rents to the priory. The case of Elizabeth Montague was exceptional: the daughter of William Lord Montague, she brought with her a pension of £5 per year in the 1330s and was soon elected prioress; one of her sisters was abbess of Barking.

Augustinian canonesses were not secluded in the way some nuns were. St Leonard's Shoreditch performed the function of a parish church, but the nuns of Holywell undertook charitable work in their local community. Holywell and other London nunneries are often referred to together as 'hospitals', suggesting they did care for the sick. Many nunneries ran schools for local children, as did St Helen's Bishopsgate in 1439. Some had connections with merchants and others through guilds and religious fraternities; the nuns prayed for the members' souls and benefited financially. Holywell was connected with the Parish Clerks' Fraternity and prioresses were regularly admitted as members in the 15th century.

A burial in the nave of the church during excavation

Two rings found in graves at Holywell Priory; that on the right has an opaque glass inset

There were men attached to the priory, who acted as rent collectors or stewards, as well as servants or labourers who assisted with everyday matters. In addition, there were the priests or chaplains who conducted the daily services and probably lived within the precinct, but away from the nuns. In the years before 1539 there were a number of non-religious people living within the precinct, in houses and gardens along the main road and south of the church; the two priests who served the Lovell chapel lived south of church.

Nuns and some of these residents and benefactors would have been buried within the precinct and some stipulated this in their wills. Henry Aubrey, steward of Holywell, asked in 1471 to be buried in the 'High Chancel' of the priory church. Sir George Manners, Lord Roos of Hamlake, requested burial near the high altar in 1513. The north side of the church in particular seems to have been a focus for later burials. Of the 30 medieval burials found during the excavations, 28 were within the church; these comprised both women and men, as well as children including new-borns. The remains of wooden coffins and a lead coffin were found. Individuals were sometimes buried dressed, rather than shrouded; a headdress pin and two rings were found with bodies at Holywell. Two burials were also excavated immediately south of the church in the cemetery situated here and to the south-east; the cemetery was walled on the east.

The end of the priory

At the Dissolution, Holywell Priory was suppressed and its property seized; in 1539 the nuns were pensioned off. Lead was taken from Holywell in 1540–1 to repair the roof of Westminster Hall. The chapter house – 'the roofe … with the selyng of waynescott, the tyle stones, the pavynge stones, the glasse, the iron and the walles' – was sold in its entirety and seems to have been pulled down by August 1541.

In 1537 the prioress had leased the houses and mansions south of the church to Thomas Earl of Rutland, the chief steward of the priory, who retained this property after 1539. Queen Katharine secured the site of the church and cloister for Henry Webb, her gentleman usher, in 1544, when the church, chapter house, dormitory and a chapel at the north end of the refectory were only 'land and soil'. Part of the former precinct (the south-west) went in 1542 to George Harper.

While most of the principal buildings of the nunnery then were quickly roofless and demolished, the rest seem to have been largely reused. By the end of the reign of Henry VIII, most of the religious precincts in London had been transferred to courtiers or Crown officials and then occupied by prestigious lodgings or mansions. The cloister of St Mary Clerkenwell became the house of the Duke of Newcastle, Holy Trinity Priory the residence of first Sir Thomas Audley and then the 4th Duke of Norfolk. A few monastic churches, like St Helen's Bishopsgate, were at least partly retained as parish churches.

Painted fragments of tomb canopy in Reigate stone, found in demolition material in the church

The Tudor mansion

*A 16th-century pottery jug in
London-area redware from the
Holywell Priory site*

of the earls of Rutland

Thomas Manners, the first Earl of Rutland, who acquired the south-west part of the former Holywell precinct was a Knight of the Garter and a great favourite of Henry VIII. He was with the king at the famous 'Field of the Cloth of Gold' in France in 1520 (a Tudor 'summit meeting'), and he took part in the trial of Queen Anne Boleyn for adultery, incest and witchcraft in 1536. Henry VIII granted Manners many estates, and he had been the steward of a number of monasteries, including Holywell Priory. After the Dissolution Manners received the lands of a number of these former monasteries, making him even wealthier.

The Manners' mansion at Holywell may have comprised a rambling collection of buildings, as it appears to have reused the existing, pre-Dissolution, 'houses and mansion'. The Agas map of c 1562 shows the gateway and a number of buildings in the southern half of the former precinct. Most of the priory buildings were knocked down. Some of the stone from demolished priory buildings may have been reused in new buildings. Two of the piers in the priory church were reduced to three or four courses in height, and appear to have been deliberately displayed as decorative stone features within a brick floor.

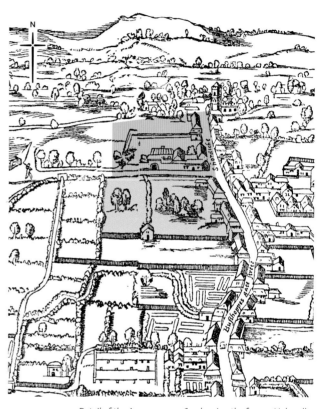

Detail of the Agas map, c 1562, showing the former Holywell Priory precinct and adjacent open land to the south

The tomb of Thomas Manners, first Earl of Rutland (d 1543), in the church of St Mary the Virgin, Bottesford, Leicestershire

27

Brick walls found in the excavations were from several of the subsidiary, service, buildings of the complex; many of these apparently continued in use for the next two centuries. One of the brick buildings had a plaster floor; it opened onto a courtyard and there were cesspits nearby.

Finds indicating the wealth of the occupants include imported floor tiles from the Netherlands, glass vessels from Venice, and Ming Dynasty Chinese porcelain – a rare archaeological find from deposits of this period. Flower seeds from the silts in a ditch suggest that columbine and pinks were grown in the gardens.

Yellow-, green- and brown-glazed Low Countries floor tiles from the Earl of Rutland's mansion

A subsidiary building of the Earl of Rutland's mansion (left); with a later courtyard surface, with reused stone from Holywell Priory, and cesspit (right)

Aristocratic living

The Earl of Rutland and his family would have entertained many guests when they were in residence at their Shoreditch manor. Holding a sumptuous banquet was an important way to impress guests, demonstrating your wealth and status with a vast array of sumptuous exotic food. The excavation produced evidence for black pepper from India, allspice from the West Indies, and grapes and figs from the Mediterranean. A variety of kitchen utensils were used to prepare the food and, at Holywell, the pottery included cauldrons, pipkins (handled cooking vessels used like saucepans), skillets and jars. The food would have been served on a variety of platters, porringers (small handled bowls for spooned foods), dishes and bowls, whilst drink was served from jugs. An unusual find was a cylindrical German stoneware tankard, decorated with double-headed eagles, probably connected with the Hanseatic League (an extremely influential trading alliance of northern European cities).

The Armada portrait of Elizabeth I shows the Queen richly dressed and adorned with precious jewels

Siegburg stoneware tankard, with the arms of the Holy Roman Empire and the date, 1582, made during the reign of Elizabeth I

Tudor aristocrats also displayed their wealth and privileged status by wearing elegant clothing, made of expensive materials such as velvet, satin, silk and furs, and costly jewellery. The king and queen would set the trend at court, as the aristocrats sought royal favour by imitating the monarch's clothing styles. In the reign of Elizabeth I, it was popular for noble women to wear corsets, bodices, petticoats and gowns, while the men wore doublets, breeches and stockings. Both sexes wore ruffs around the neck and wrists, collars, hats and buckled leather shoes. The poorer classes wore much more simple clothes, made from cheaper materials.

Finds from the Holywell Priory site include a large number of pieces from leather shoes, copper-alloy shoe buckles, and a bodkin for use in sewing such tough materials, together with three 16th-century rings, possibly curtain rings.

Copper-alloy ?curtain rings from the Earl of Rutland's mansion

The Great House

and the Stone House

Whilst the priory was flourishing to the west of Shoreditch High Street, the occupation lining the eastern edge of the medieval road gradually expanded. Tantalisingly, the houses themselves seem to have lain just west of Bishopsgate Goods Yard site, because the current road has been widened since the medieval period. Within the site, the digging of pits for refuse, small-scale brickearth extraction and a few wells were found, in what were the gardens and backyards of buildings that lined the medieval road. Pit fills dated to *c* 1350–1500 contained personal items including shoe buckles, coins (medieval jettons) and hones, for sharpening knives or other tools, made of schist (a hard stone imported from Norway). A lead weight, weighing 48g (about 2oz), may have been used by a tradesman or merchant, and a small amount of copper waste suggests that metal might have been cast in the area.

The earliest remains of buildings found at Bishopsgate Goods Yard were also located in this area, and may form part of a large house called the *Great House*, known to have occupied the southern portion of the original Shoreditch High Street frontage here. It was in existence by the middle of the 16th century, as it appears to be shown on the Agas map of *c* 1562, but may have been constructed in the previous century. Alternatively, the remains may have been associated with another building to the east, known as the *Stone House* and also probably shown on the Agas map.

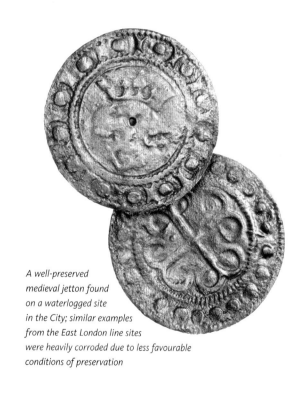

A well-preserved medieval jetton found on a waterlogged site in the City; similar examples from the East London line sites were heavily corroded due to less favourable conditions of preservation

Detail from the Agas map 1562, showing a large building (highlightded in orange), east of Shoreditch High Street, that may be the Great House

A late medieval composite buckle from the Bishopsgate Goods Yard site

The base of a large 16th-century bread oven, possibly associated with the Great House, *with a brick working-surface to the rear*

31

Building remains included a possible cellar structure with floor, located on the Shoreditch High Street frontage and using bricks dated to *c* 1450–1600. One of the walls included an area of different coloured bricks laid in the popular Tudor 'diamond diaper' pattern, alongside general walling bricks laid horizontally. Other structures possibly associated with the Great House include brick-lined cesspits (again with bricks dated to *c* 1450–1600), rubbish pits and what appears to have been a very large, brick-walled bread oven, some 2m across. The oven floor consisted of a central, heavily fired, ragstone block (that bore evidence of having been subjected to intense heat), surrounded by a radiating arrangement of roofing tiles set on edge to resist the high temperatures. A small brick surface probably represents an adjacent working area. The oven may have belonged to the kitchens of the *Great House*.

The finds associated with the demolition of these buildings suggest that these buildings were indeed of high status. They include glazed and unglazed floor tiles imported from the Low Countries (Holland and Belgium) in the 15th and early 16th centuries. These tiles had a plain yellow, green or brown glaze and would have been laid in a chequerboard pattern. The demolition material included finds which may date to the 15th century or earlier.

Tudor building, possibly part of the Great House, *with original brick floor and later 17th-century joist holes for a replacement wooden floor*

A reconstructed Tudor kitchen including a bread oven similar to (but smaller than) the one found at the Bishopsgate Goods Yard site

A very fine piece of worked and decorated greensand (stone) with traces of gilding and paint on its surface was also discovered. It may have originated from the Great House and originally have been used as a fireplace or window surround. It is thought to date from the late 16th century, and it is possible that the design was inspired by Hans Vredeman de Vries's book *Architectura* which was published in 1565. De Vries was known as the 'Leonardo Da Vinci of the Low Countries'. It was discovered face down, incorporated in an early 19th-century yard surface.

The decorated greensand frieze undergoing conservation work; due to its fragile condition it was lifted in its block of surrounding soil and then cleaned in the laboratory

A 16th-century jug in Surrey-Hampshire border ware from the Holywell Priory site

Detail from the greensand frieze after cleaning and conservation work

Bricks, brickearth

and Brick Lane

The area around Shoreditch station today gives no hint of the activities related to brick production that were undertaken on the site. One exception is the aptly named Brick Lane, so-called from the 17th century, if not before. In fact, brickearth extraction and brick production was one of the main activities carried out in the area until the late 1600s. Small-scale brickearth extraction was also being undertaken from at least the 14th century.

The production of bricks was hugely important in the development of London as we know it today, and many areas across London were quarried for brickearth to make bricks and tiles from Roman times to the Victorian period.

Some of the quarries that were investigated at Bishopsgate Goods Yard were large trenches – over 10m long, 3m wide and 2m deep. Nearby hoof prints and cart ruts represent this material being hauled to nearby brick kilns or clamps. At least one of the quarries has been dated to immediately after the Great Fire of London in 1666; it had been filled in with what appears to be debris from the Great Fire itself. With that in mind, it can be said with some certainty that the quarry helped in the rebuilding of the City of London, or at least the expansion of the suburbs, perhaps on the Bishopsgate Goods Yard site itself.

Once the brickearth had been used up, the quarries were then filled in, the ground levelled, and then these areas too were engulfed by the suburban development they had helped to create. This process of quarrying, quarry infilling, brick production and subsequent development continued until London reached the extent that we see today.

The Brick Lane street sign; the name, whose origins relate to the manufacture of bricks, can be traced back to at least the 17th century

Excavation of a brickearth quarry at the east end of the Bishopsgate Goods Yard site, close to Brick Lane

London going out of town ... or ... The march of bricks and mortar *by George Cruickshank (1829) was a satirical take on the expansion of London's suburbs. Its less than favourable imagery shows brick clamps spewing hot bricks into the retreating countryside, the digging of brickearth and the felling of trees, as well as the encroaching pollution from the city of London. Not only does it illustrate the processes involved in suburban development but it also serves as an early example of a satirical illustration of the impact of urban expansion on the rural environment*

Despite the obvious advantage of using brick (strength, durability), it was actually made a legal requirement by an Act of Parliament in February 1667 which stated 'that the outsides of buildings be henceforth made of brick or stone'. This was a measure to avoid any repeat of the Great Fire.

Brickearth extraction was a seasonal activity, with the clay traditionally being dug in the autumn, weathered overwinter, tempered in the early spring and made into bricks in the late spring, summer and early autumn. When the clay had been extracted, left to weather, mixed with water, turned over and stones removed and any tempering material added, it was made into the traditional brick shape by use of a wooden mould pressed into a 'clot' of finished clay. Excess clay was then removed with a stick or wire. Once this was done the bricks were then fired in either a brick kiln or a temporary kiln known as a brick clamp. Evidence for these was found at Bishopsgate Goods Yard, and also at the Hoxton station site, in the form of a large area of burning of the underlying soil, with brick waste and deposits of clay and charcoal.

A brick clamp was a temporary, single-use, kiln-structure made by stacking up the 'green' (unfired) bricks into a roughly square structure, tapering inwards towards the top. Brick clamps varied in size, but there could have been up to 150,000 bricks in just one clamp. The lowest levels of bricks were arranged with gaps between them; these channels were filled with wood, and further fuel was interspersed in the lower courses. Once ignited, they could take 2–12 weeks to burn, depending on size. When fully burnt they were then dismantled, and usable bricks kept and later transported away from the clamp. Debris from spoiled bricks was also found during the excavations.

A brief history of the brick

Bricks have been used in this country since Roman times. Following the end of the Roman period there was a hiatus in the use of brick. It was not until the later medieval period (from *c* AD 1400) that bricks were again regularly used in England. Initially, they were used for fireplaces in otherwise inflammable timber buildings, but increased in popularity when they were used in aristocratic great houses, such as Hampton Court or Lambeth Palace. It is possible to date bricks by their size, composition (temper and clay) and other features such as mould marks, or 'frogs'.

Frog – the indentation moulded into the base of bricks from the 18th century onwards, to help key the bricks to the mortar and thus the rest of the wall.

Green brick – an unfired moulded brick.

Temper – material mixed into the clay: early bricks might have grit or even pieces of clay tobacco pipe added to save on clay; later bricks might have sand or straw, to aid in firing the bricks, which burnt out, leaving holes.

A chronology of London bricks (from top): a medieval brick, a Tudor brick, an 18th-century brick and a 19th-century brick

Brickfields by C H Matthews, c 1830, showing the entire process of brick production in Dalston, with quarrying, drying-out of the green bricks and the construction and firing of the brick clamps

Eastenders – suburban

17th-century Bartmann *(bearded man) jugs in Frechen stoneware from a cesspit on the Bishopsgate Goods Yard site*

development in the 17th century

While a settlement had existed from the medieval period alongside what is now Shoreditch High Street, the land to the east remained open fields, still shown on a map of 1658. It was not until the late 17th century that we see development further to the east across the Bishopsgate Goods Yard site, to Brick Lane and beyond. The old City became increasingly crowded and, although there had been some ribbon development of housing lining the streets leading out from the City, there were opportunities for development in the fields beyond. The redevelopment of land around Spitalfields and Shoreditch was started by Sir George Wheler in the late 17th century.

The rapidly expanding population was the main catalyst for this development and expansion of London's suburbs. Not only were people drawn to London from other parts of Britain, such as East Anglia or Ireland, but also large numbers of people from abroad settled here, many in east London. By the time Morgan mapped the area in 1682, the suburban townscape was well established, with houses, yards and streets occupying all of the area between Shoreditch High Street and Brick Lane.

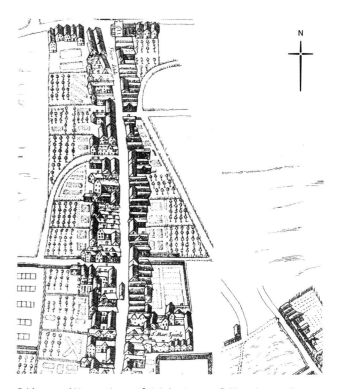

Faithorne and Newcourt's map of 1658 showing open fields to the east of Shoreditch High Street

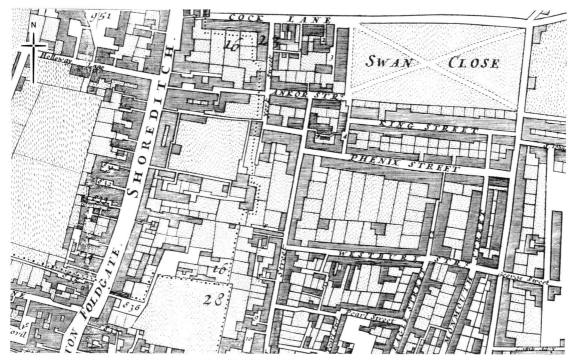

Morgan's map of 1682 showing the development of a suburban landscape by the late 17th century

The base of a 17th-century brick-lined cesspit excavated on the Bishopsgate Goods Yard site

Dutch tin-glazed ('Delft') tiles
from the Bishopsgate Goods Yard site:
a mounted military figure, c 1625–60,
and a seated man and cockerel, c 1650–80

17th-century pottery vessels from the
Bishopsgate Goods Yard site (from left):
a Surrey-Hampshire border whiteware
chamber pot and tin-glazed ware
('delftware') dish and porringer

This change over only 20 years, from an open landscape of fields and quarrying to suburban sprawl, would have been dramatic. Prior to development, large quantities of material, thought to be debris from the Great Fire of 1666, was dumped on parts of the site to raise the ground level, to create building platforms and to fill in brickearth quarries. These deposits, up to 1m deep, represent part of a formidable undertaking in clearing the areas destroyed by the Fire.

The excavations on the Bishopsgate Goods Yard site showed that the late 17th-century buildings were constructed from brick, no doubt locally made, and the roofs were covered with either peg tiles or pantiles. In one 17th-century cellar excavated at Bishopsgate Goods Yard, a large pottery vessel was buried flush with the brick floor, and is thought to be a soakaway (for drainage). Delftware tiles, a large number of which were found on the site, are likely to have been used to decorate the surrounds of the fireplaces within these buildings, as well as the kitchens. Where not disturbed by later construction, the buildings exhibited a succession of internal floors and external yard surfaces – in brick, stone or wood – as well as rebuilding and alterations to their walls.

Most of the structures excavated belonged to the cellars of these houses. In the yard areas of some of the properties were found wells (some of which were lined with wooden barrels), soakaways and, most commonly, cesspits which were lined with bricks. With no flushing toilets until the late 19th century, chamber pots were emptied into cesspits, or the street! Cesspits are particularly useful for clues to the lifestyle of the people living in the adjacent buildings, as they often contain well-preserved food remains, and even parasites that had troubled the inhabitants, as well as large quantities of finds, especially pottery vessels, thrown away as rubbish.

17th-century pottery vessels from the Holywell Priory site (from top): a Rhenish stoneware jug, two Surrey-Hampshire border whiteware money boxes and a redware candle holder

41

in the 18th century

The 18th century saw the consolidation of the urban landscape which had expanded across the Bishopsgate Goods Yard site in the previous century, and its subsequent degradation. Whilst known as the 'age of enlightenment', life for ordinary Londoners in the 18th century could be very hard.

As the century progressed, the artisans and tradesmen who lived and worked there found that their boom time was turning to bust. One example of this was the silk weavers who found themselves unable to compete with the more mechanised weaving techniques that were being introduced. This caused a certain amount of unrest, and on more than one occasion angry mobs took to Shoreditch High Street in protest.

Despite the tentative steps to the more modern society we are familiar with today, there was a steady increase in poverty and a decrease in the standard of living conditions, especially in East London. These factors culminated in the Victorian slums of the 19th century.

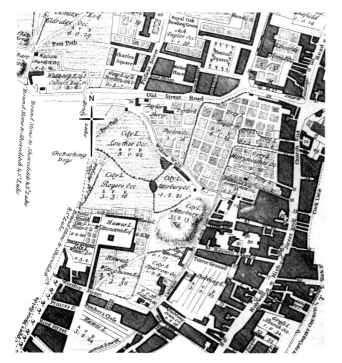

A bird's-eye view of the excavation trench alongside Shoreditch High Street and the remains of 18th-century buildings on the Bishopsgate Goods Yard site

Chassereau's map of 1745 showing Shoreditch (here Holywell) High Street (right)

43

Archaeologists cleaning an 18th-century floor surface on the Bishopsgate Goods Yard site alongside Shoreditch High Street frontage

The buildings

Ramshackle buildings, overcrowding and poverty became common features of this part of London. Rather than individual families living in separate properties, it was common practice for a family to cook, eat and live in a single room. A whole family would share one bed. Warrens of illegal buildings sprang up in areas where they could be concealed from the authorities. Often cellars were excavated to provide more accommodation; such rooms would have little or no natural light. Human waste was still deposited in cesspits, usually located in the yards of the houses, as there was no other sanitation, and no running water system.

A number of these buildings with associated yard surfaces and cesspits were recorded during the excavations on both the Bishopsgate Goods Yard and Holywell Priory sites. Their yards had brick surfaces and dividing walls, cesspits, soakaways, drains and rubbish pits. One cesspit at the Holywell Priory site contained 90 chamber pots – it has not yet been determined what the owners were doing with so many of these essential, if unprepossessing, items.

Many of the everyday items used within these buildings were found during the investigations. These included chamber pots, cooking vessels, plates, drinking vessels and even bone toothbrushes.

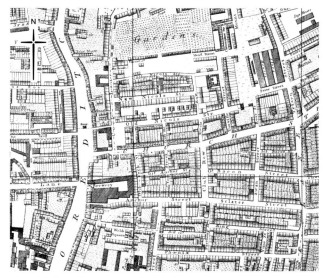

Horwood's map of 1799 showing the fully developed suburban landscape across this part of East London at the end of the 18th century

18th-century tin-glazed tiles from the Bishopsgate Goods Yard site (from top): made in London, c 1740–60; Dutch, c 1680–1800; London, c 1740–60

Excavating the interior of an 18th-century building on the Bishopsgate Goods Yard site

Furnace base dating to the 18th century which was found in one of the buildings on the Shoreditch High Street frontage

Food and diet

Analysis of the cesspit fills associated with 18th-century buildings on the Bishopsgate Goods Yard and Holywell Priory sites has provided information about the diet of the people in this part of East London. It included ox, lamb or mutton, as well as duck, chicken, herring, plaice or flounder and cod. The bones of the larger animals often exhibit knife-marks from butchery of the carcass.

Dish or platter with slip decoration in Surrey-Hampshire border redware

Industry

The crowded living conditions were exacerbated by various trades and small-scale industry undertaken within the same buildings. A smithy with the base of a small furnace was found in one of the properties which fronted onto Shoreditch High Street. Tiny fragments of metal ('hammerscale') were found in the area around it, along with lumps of slag that had accumulated in such furnaces or hearths, demonstrating that it had been used for ironworking.

Evidence for other small-scale industries included pottery vessels called cucurbits for distilling strong acids, and fragments of moulds and syrup collecting jars for processing sugar imported from the plantations in the West Indies. There were also finds indicating glass working, ivory and bone working and textile making in the area.

An 18th-century brick-lined cesspit on the Holywell Priory site

A group of sugar refining vessels – many fragments of similar vessels were found in one of the 18th-century buildings on the Bishopsgate Goods Yard site

Leisure

As well as sports that are still practised today, such as cricket, football and boxing, animal baiting with dogs was extremely popular in the 18th century. Creatures as diverse as bulls, bears and badgers were considered suitable game for these somewhat cruel 'sporting events'. Cock fighting was also enjoyed by the masses.

A less brutal pastime, still played to this day, was marbles, and the Bishopsgate Goods Yard site has produced one of the largest collections of 18th- and 19th-century marbles or allies yet found in London.

Marble allies from the Bishopsgate Goods Yard site

Tom 'The Disher' Juchau

Documentary research has shown that an object from Bishopsgate Goods Yard provides a direct link to 18th-century leisure activities, more specifically bare-knuckle boxing. The object was a small curved copper-alloy plate on which was inscribed 'Thos Juchau / Shoreditch'.

Thomas Juchau was born 25 December 1739 in St Giles in the Field, Holborn, and was a paviour by trade. He was said to have been the 'hero of a hundred fights', although only two of those were recorded. He became the bare-knuckle-fighting champion in 1765 and held the title for two years until he was defeated by William 'the dyer' Darts, who was a Spitalfields dyer. This bout was credited as being the first outdoor heavyweight boxing match and, after losing the title, Thomas never fought again. He died in 1806 by which time he was living on Batemans Row, St Leonards, Shoreditch.

The bruising match by Hemskerk (c 1760), showing bare-knuckle boxing

It has not yet been possible to identify the exact function of the object, although it was presumably mounted on a leather strap and was probably attached to one of his possessions, perhaps even adorning a dog collar.

A curved copper-alloy mount inscribed 'Thos Juchau / Shoreditch'

Whilst Thomas achieved immortality with regards to his bare-knuckle exploits, his younger brother Philip, a coachman and also an aspiring boxer, was not so lucky. He was killed during a bare-knuckle contest with a butcher named Jack Warren outside Bethlem Gates, Moorfields, in 1765.

Smoking and drinking

Some less healthy leisure pursuits, such as smoking and drinking, were also extremely common during this period. Tobacco was smoked in clay pipes; thousands of fragments of these were found during the archaeological excavations. They were relatively cheap, mass-produced items, and their rapidly-changing styles form a useful tool for archaeologists to determine the date of deposits in which they are found. As the 18th century progressed, the bowls of the pipes became decorated. Some of these advertised local pubs and taverns, whilst others had designs depicting significant persons and events, such as the Admiral Vernon pipe (right).

Drinking was a very common pastime in the 18th century. Weak beer was drunk in place of water, as it was generally much safer; but it was a different story for spirits, or more specifically ... gin! The consumption of gin was a huge problem in London during the first half of the 18th century amongst the city's poor and its use/abuse reached epidemic proportions. It is thought that over 9000 children died from the effects of gin in 1751 alone. The effects of it upon the person and society are well illustrated in Hogarth's *Gin Lane* engraving.

Hogarth's Gin Lane – *a shocking illustration of the effects of gin on the London population*

'Grog' Vernon and Portobello – the man, the pipe, the rum and the road

This highly decorated clay tobacco pipe was found in a cesspit on the Bishopsgate Goods Yard site. It commemorates an admiral and a victory long forgotten, yet whose names still faintly echo today.

The pipe bowl depicts Admiral Vernon on one side and, on the other, kneeling in surrender, Don Blas de Leso, the Spanish governor of the city of Cartagena in Panama. On the front is one of the British warships from Vernon's victorious fleet.

Edward Vernon has two claims to fame. Firstly, he introduced to the navy the daily rum-ration of 'grog', watered-down rum, which earned him the nick-name 'Grog' Vernon. Secondly, he commanded a fleet in the Caribbean during the oddly-named *War of Jenkin's Ear*. Whether or not Spanish coastguards had actually cut off one ear of the English Captain Robert Jenkins, it served as a reason for war with Spain, in which Vernon's fleet captured Porto Bello in Panama in 1739. The song *Rule Britannia* was written to commemorate his triumph.

Two years later, although Vernon's ships destroyed the Spanish squadron at Cartagena, the army failed to take the city itself. The admiral, however, had been so confident of victory that, before the event, he had medals made showing the Spanish governor kneeling in surrender. This pipe also depicts this image, despite the fact that it never happened! Nevertheless, Admiral Vernon became a popular hero of the time, was made a freeman of the City of London, and places in London, Edinburgh and Dublin were named Portobello after his capture of the lucrative Spanish trading centre.

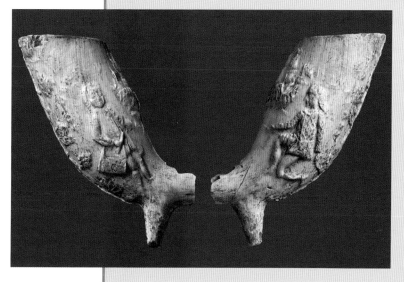

A witch bottle and a witch box

The witch hunts that took place across Europe during the 16th and 17th centuries resulted in a widespread fear of witches and increased superstition. People believed that witches could enter a house through the doors, windows or chimneys, and in order to protect their family they hid witch bottles in these places. This was thought to protect the household by placing a curse on the witch. A bottle or jug, generally made of stoneware from the Rhineland and known today as a *Bartmann* ('bearded man'), was used as the container. It was filled with items intended to ward off a curse, including bent copper pins, human hair and urine. A witch bottle was discovered at the Holywell Lane site, hidden beneath the brick floor of a house sometime between 1700 and 1740. It is unusual in being made from London stoneware and without the customary bearded face. Such vessels were made in the last quarter of the 17th century in imitation of Rhenish wares.

Witch bottles were not the only charms used to combat witches and malevolent spirits. Also popular, but far less common in the archaeological record, were 'witch boxes', which similarly contained a variety of materials believed to counteract witches' spells. These are recorded as being sold by the witch finders during the witch hunts, in what could be seen as a clever piece of marketing. The wooden box found at the Bishopsgate Goods Yard had been inserted in place of a brick during the construction of a fireplace in the 18th century. Inside had been placed assorted animal bones, including sheep or goat, pig and goose.

The London stoneware jug from the Holywell Priory site used as a witch bottle, with the bent pins which were placed inside it

The 18th-century building in which the witch box was found

The witch box – an assortment of animal bone in a wooden box concealed in a fireplace during the construction of a building on the Bishopsgate Goods Yard site

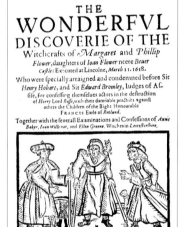

THE
WONDERFVL
DISCOVERIE OF THE
Witchcrafts of *Margaret* and *Phillip*
Flower, daughters of *Ioan Flower* neere *Beuer*
Caſtle: Executed at Lincolne, *March* 11. 1618.
Who were ſpecially arraigned and condemned before Sir
Henry Hobart, and Sir *Edward Bromley*, Iudges of Aſ-
ſiſe, for confeſſing themſelues actors in the deſtruction
of *Henry Lord Roſſe*, with their damnable practiſes againſt
others the Children of the Right Honourable
FRANCIS Earle of *Rutland*.
Together with the ſeuerall Examinations and Confeſſions of *Anne
Baker, Ioan Willimot*, and *Ellen Greene*, Witches in *Leiceſterſhire*.

Printed at London by *G. Eld* for *I. Barnes*, dwelling in the long Walke
neere Chriſt-Church. 1 6 1 9.

Wood engraving from a pamphlet describing a famous early 17th-century witch trial

A descendant of the original Earl of Rutland, builder of the Tudor mansion on the site of Holywell Priory, was involved in this trial. Francis Manners, the 6th Earl of Rutland, of Belvoir Castle, Lincolnshire, accused six women of witchcraft after the premature death of his two sons. The fates of three of the accused were unrecorded, but Joan Flower died in prison and her two daughters, Margaret and Philippa, were burned at the stake in Lincoln on 11 March 1618/19.

The case was commemorated on the Earl's tomb in St Mary's Church Bottesford; an inscription stated that his two sons 'died in their infancy by wicked practises and sorcerye'.

The origins and construction

of the East London line

The East London line has its roots in the construction of a tunnel beneath the River Thames between 1825 and 1843 by the French-born engineer Sir Marc Isambard Brunel, and his son Isambard Kingdom Brunel. In the early 19th century a new land link was needed between the rapidly expanding docks in Wapping and Rotherhithe. A number of unsuccessful attempts had been made to construct a tunnel under the Thames, but the Brunels were the first to achieve it, although they were hampered by lack of funds and by tunnel collapses. In the end, the tunnel cost £454,000 to excavate, and a further £180,000 to fit out with lighting, roads and staircases at either end.

The entrance to the Thames Tunnel at Wapping, in 1836 (print produced before completion when the tunnel was expected to be used by horse-drawn vehicles)

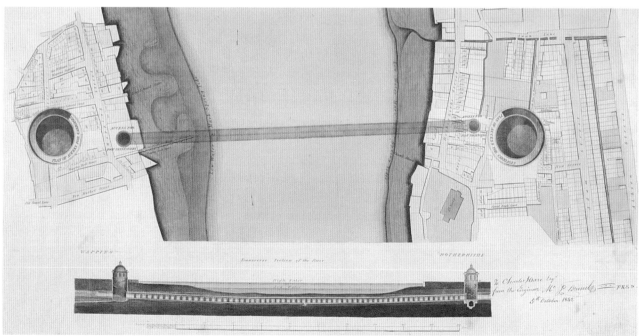

Plan and longitudinal section of the Thames Tunnel from 1842

A view along the Thames Tunnel , c 1835

The platforms at Wapping station in 1870

Wapping station in 1936

It had been intended that vehicles should be able to use the tunnel, but as a cost-saving measure the ramps that horses would have required were not built. The tunnel was opened with great fanfare, and the American traveller William Allen Drew described it as the eighth wonder of the world. There were shops and stalls selling souvenirs along the length of the tunnel, but the shine soon wore off and the tunnel became a haunt for thieves and prostitutes.

In 1865 the Thames Tunnel was purchased for the sum of £800,000 by the East London Railway Company, a consortium of six railway companies. The company wanted to use it as a link between Wapping and the rail network in south London. The first stations were opened in 1869 at Wapping, Rotherhithe, Deptford Road (later renamed Surrey Dock, then Surrey Quays) and New Cross (renamed New Cross Gate in 1923). The line was then extended to Shoreditch in 1876, with stations at Whitechapel and Shadwell.

The East London Railway came under the control of the London Underground in 1933, and some of the stations were later improved or rebuilt. Wapping station was almost entirely rebuilt after being hit, like much of the docks, by bombing during the Second World War.

The East London Railway, shown on the Map of the electric railways of London *of 1915*

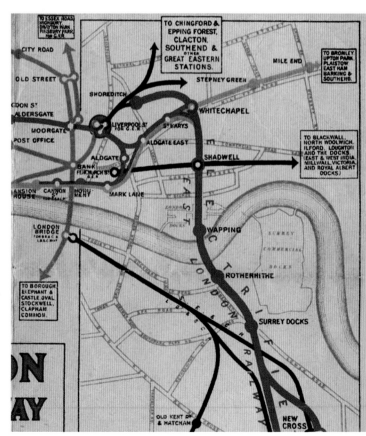

Excerpt from the London bomb damage map from the Second World War, showing the devastation caused to the area around Wapping station (darker coloured buildings were badly damaged or destroyed)

Wapping station was badly damaged during an air raid on 11 September 1940

The staff of the London Underground took great pride in keeping their stations neat and tidy; here Mrs Metherall, the station porter at Shoreditch, is being awarded third prize in a gardening competition

The ticket office at Shoreditch station

In 1983 a new station was opened at Shadwell; the old station buildings still stand today

The Great

Eastern Railway

Until the 1830s most railways which had been constructed in Britain were for the transportation of goods; the Liverpool & Manchester Railway, which opened in 1830, ran one of the earliest services intended purely for passenger trains. During the 1830s a kind of 'railway mania' gripped the nation – investors ploughed money into the construction of railways, attracted by the potential for massive profits in schemes that would transform the way in which goods and people moved around the country. Until the mid 19th century, long-distance travel around the country was mostly undertaken by a network of horse-drawn stage coaches, which could only carry passengers and light goods. Heavy goods were transported by water, on river boats or coastal barges, and, from the 1760s, by the increasing network of

canals. Not all of the planned railways were constructed: 40% of the railway lines authorised by Parliament were never built, and some schemes were promoted by unscrupulous companies promising quick returns on investments with no intention of following through with their plans.

The earliest passenger railway to be constructed in the capital was the London & Greenwich Railway, the first stretch of which opened in February 1836. It provided a speedy link between the eastern suburbs on the southern bank of the Thames, but the first railway to connect the capital with the greater part of the country was the London & Birmingham Railway, which opened its terminus at Euston in 1837, followed by the Great Western Railway to Bristol, which opened at Paddington in 1838.

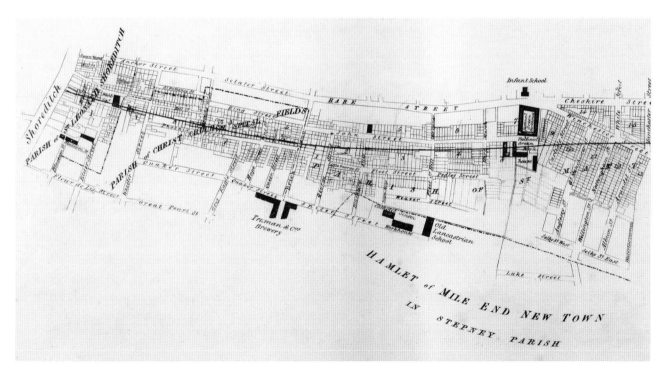

An 1835 map of the route of the Eastern Counties Railway through Shoreditch and Spitalfields

The Bishopsgate terminus in Shoreditch High Street in 1850

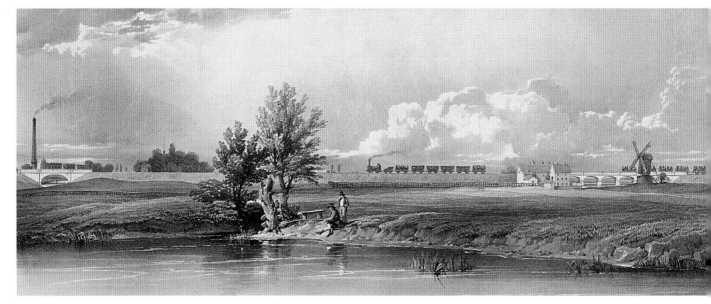

The plans for the Eastern Counties Railway line from London to Norwich were prepared in the early 1830s, and a prospectus for potential investors was published in 1834. There were a number of possible locations for the London terminus, including sites in Bethnal Green, Shoreditch High Street, the junction of Bishopsgate and Norton Folgate, Islington Cattle Market, and a site adjacent to Brick Lane. The minutes of a meeting of the Provisional Committee for the construction of the railway from October 1835 recorded that a survey of the area had been made:

From a point adjacent to Brick Lane, where it was originally proposed that the Eastern Counties Railway should terminate, as far forward as High Street, Shoreditch, for a breadth of two hundred feet, that this space included no more than 373 houses of which 140 were very old and consisted of two rooms and let to weekly tenants at sums varying from 2/6d to 3/6d each. 130 are four and five roomed houses in a most ruinous state. 50 are larger but equally ruinous and not much more than 30 are in a good state of repair or of much value (Minutes of the Provisional Committee of the Eastern Counties Railway, 22 October 1835).

The Bill for the line's construction was presented to Parliament in February 1836 and was passed in July of that year, after stiff opposition from landowners and the promoters of two rival railway schemes. Construction of the railway began soon after and the first section, between Mile End and Romford, opened in 1839. The stretch of line between Mile End and the terminus in Shoreditch High Street opened the following year, and the rest of the line, between Romford and Norwich, opened in stages. Much of the railway was constructed through agricultural land, and where it crossed the marshy ground around Stratford, to the east of London, it was raised on an earth embankment. A brick viaduct, a mile and a quarter (*c* 2km) in length and containing 160 arches, was constructed to carry the railway through the crowded streets of the East End to the terminus in Shoreditch (the station was renamed as 'Bishopsgate' in 1847). Although it was costly to build, the vertical-sided structure would have a smaller footprint than an embankment, reducing the number of buildings which needed to be demolished, and also providing a series of arches which could be let out at a profit.

The railway arches in Pedley Street

A railwayman at the Great Eastern Railway Company's Horse Infirmary in Pedley Street, c 1911, demonstrating the level of injuries to the company's horses; nails recovered from their hooves were hung in strips of leather each year

In 1862 the Eastern Counties Railway merged with a number of smaller companies, which also ran railway lines in East Anglia, to form the Great Eastern Railway (GER). At around this time the viaduct which led to Bishopsgate station in Shoreditch High Street was widened on its northern side to accommodate the increasing number of trains that were using the line. The arches in Pedley Street, to the east of Brick Lane, had been open to the street, but the opportunity was taken to convert them into usable spaces; walls with openings for doors and windows were built across the open ends and a cobbled yard was constructed on the northern side of the viaduct.

The arches in Pedley Street were subsequently used as the Great Eastern Railway Company's Horse Infirmary, where some of the company's 6000 horses were nursed back to health when they became ill or injured. Individual stalls and tethering rings for the horses were inserted underneath the arches, which had brick floors with central drains so that the stabling could be kept clean. Several of the arches had hearths for the farriers who shod the horses.

It may seem odd that a company running the new steam railway technology should require so many animals. However, once the goods were off-loaded from trains, horse-drawn transport was still the only way to distribute them from the railhead to their various destinations. Horses were, therefore, widely used by the GER to transport goods to and from its stations, and at small rural stations they often shunted the carriages and wagons. In 1865 a new horse cost £38 and 10 shillings, the equivalent of £2690 today; on average the useful working life of a horse owned by the GER was two years, before it was sold on, either to pull light carts or for slaughter.

A sludge house built in the early 20th century to supply the steam boilers of locomotives with softened water

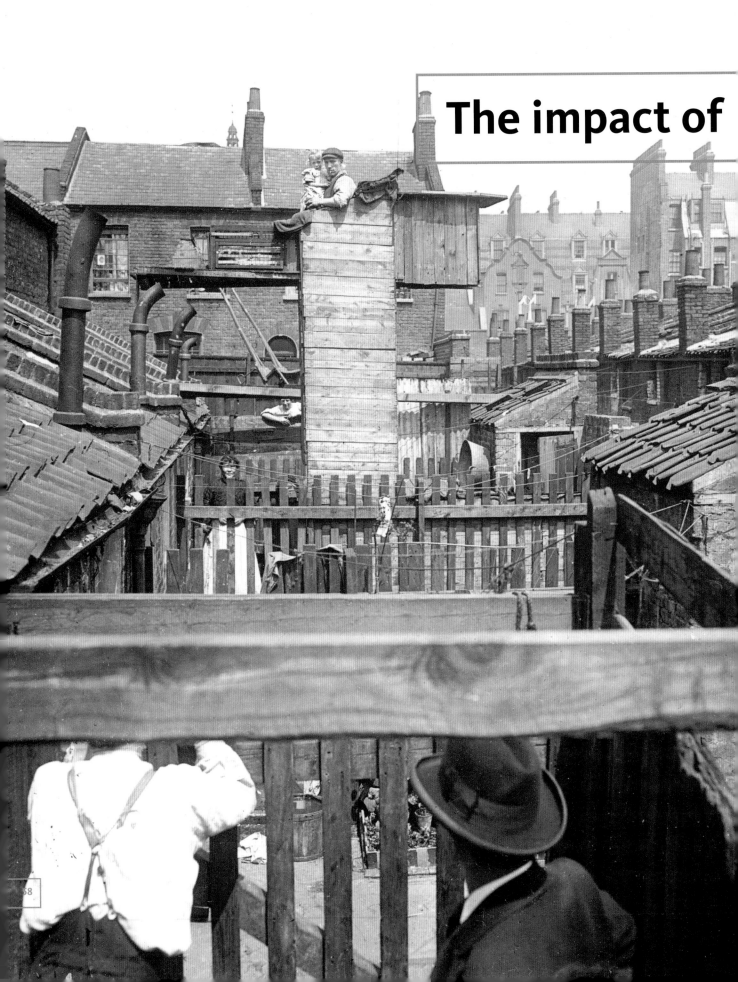

the railway on Shoreditch

The construction of the Bishopsgate terminus and the railway viaduct had an immense impact on Shoreditch. By the 1830s, many of the once-grand houses constructed in the vicinity of Shoreditch High Street had been subdivided into tenements, and additional housing or industrial premises constructed over the back gardens. We have already heard the (admittedly biased) account of the Provisional Committee of the Eastern Counties Railway of the quality of housing in the area, but there were still some open areas containing market gardens to the east of Brick Lane.

The construction of the railway terminus and viaduct cut through a number of streets, yards and alleys, and led to the demolition of hundreds of homes and workshops. The owners of affected properties were compensated for their loss, but tenants were not and there were no formal arrangements in place for the replacement of lost housing. More people were also attracted into the area looking for work on the railway, further adding to the already crowded housing situation.

In 1886, Charles Booth, a philanthropist and social campaigner who made his money from shipping and glove making, began a survey of living and working conditions in London, a project that continued until 1903. The results of the survey undertaken by Booth and his team of researchers were expressed in his *Descriptive map of London poverty*, which used a system of colour-coding residential properties to identify the economic and social makeup of each street in London. Booth's study indicated that economically mixed households were concentrated along the main roads, including Shoreditch High Street and Brick Lane, but the area through which the Great Eastern Railway passed was mainly occupied by poor and very poor families. One of Booth's investigators commented on the dirty appearance of the children in Fleet Street (now the western end of Pedley Street) and that he saw one child who was wearing only one shoe. Booth drew attention to the effect of massive physical barriers, such as railway viaducts, canals and factories, on where the poor areas of the city were located; to the north of Shoreditch 'another dark spot of long-standing poverty and extremely low life ... is wedged in between the Regent's Canal and the gas works'.

Through the endeavours of Charles Booth and other social campaigners, such as the Salvation Army, efforts were made to improve living conditions for the poor in the East End. The Old Nichol area, to the north of Bishopsgate station, was presented in contemporary newspaper accounts, and thinly disguised in fiction, as a notorious slum, the haunt of thieves and prostitutes. Between 1890 and 1900 the housing around Old Nichol Street was demolished, and the London County Council built one of the earliest social housing schemes, the Boundary Estate.

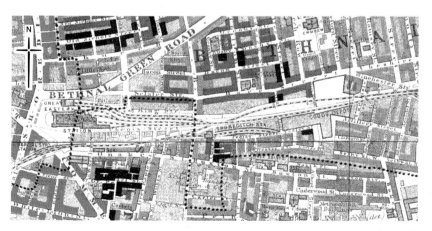

Extract from one of Charles Booth's late 19th-century maps of London poverty showing the area round Brick Lane and Pedley Street; properties in red were occupied by the prosperous middle classes and those in blue by the very poor; those in black were inhabited by the lowest social class, the 'vicious and semi-criminal'

The backyards of housing in Spitalfields, close to the Great Eastern Railway

TO THE GRILL ROOM

Goods Yard

As London, and the number of trains it needed to transport people and products, continued to expand during the 1860s, it was found that the Bishopsgate passenger terminus in Shoreditch High Street was too small and too far away from the commercial heart of London. The Great Eastern Railway line was extended into the City, and a new station, which opened in 1874, was built in Liverpool Street. After Liverpool Street station opened, the old terminus in Shoreditch High Street was closed and the site was redeveloped as Bishopsgate Goods Yard. The viaduct which carried trains into the passenger terminus was retained, and to the north and west more arches were built, which carried additional railway lines.

Above the railway lines was a third level, with 158,000 square feet of warehousing for the storage of the goods that were brought into the station. A ramp on the northern side of the station brought horse-drawn carts up to platform level, allowing goods to be loaded straight onto vehicles and taken away. A number of hydraulic lifts also enabled goods to be taken up to the warehouse or down into the railway arches, at least some of which were let out to businesses with a connection to the goods yard. The Post Office Street Directory from 1895 lists bottle manufacturers and a potato merchant in the arches underneath the goods yard, and other related businesses were located nearby in Wheler Street, including barrow makers and wine coopers.

In the period after the Second World War, the number of journeys made on Britain's railways went into decline, as more goods and people were carried on the improving road network. There was less of a need for a large goods yards like that at Bishopsgate; the final nail in its coffin occurred when the warehouse level was destroyed by fire in December 1964.

Ordnance Survey map from 1872 showing how the area to the south of Bishopsgate station was cleared in preparation for the extension of the railway to Liverpool Street

Bishopsgate Goods Yard after the fire in December 1964

The entrance to Bishopsgate Goods Yard

Liverpool Street station, 1920

Life after the

railways in Shoreditch

With the closure of the Bishopsgate Goods Yard in 1964, and of Spitalfields goods station, to the east of Fleet Street Hill, in 1967, a major contribution to the economic and social life of the area disappeared. The Great Eastern Railway Company's Horse Infirmary had long since departed the arches in Pedley Street, but there was an opportunity for the viaduct and the goods yard to find a new use. The arches provided huge spaces at little cost; there were few restrictions on the activities that could take place in the arches and little enforcement of the few rules that were in place.

Railway arches had long provided places of refuge; during the Second World War, many were converted for use as air raid shelters, and they also provided shelter for the East End's homeless. Local resident and reformed petty criminal Arthur Harding recalled the nights spent sleeping under the viaduct as a child in the 1900s:

We got slung out of Drysdale Street because we were three children, and a fourth coming, and there wasn't supposed to be any at all ... It was rainy, a January day. The first night we were homeless and settled down under Brick Lane arch for the night. There were others laying there, with sheets of newspaper on the pavement and old coats to cover them. It was a common thing both at Brick Lane arch and Wheler Street, the two railway arches. The Wheler Street arch was more crowded because it was longer and bigger. The police walked down the right-hand side, the people slept on the left.

In Pedley Street and Grimsby Street some of the arches were used by people working in the furniture trade, a long-standing industry in this part of east London. There had been a number of large factories where cheap furniture was made, but also many more smaller workshops, timber merchants, metal workers and warehouses, adding up to a kind of production line which weaved its way through the streets.

The seclusion offered by the railway arches has led to them being used for more illicit activities, especially graffiti. Grimsby Street in particular was described by the graffiti artist Banksy as 'a bulletin board for a community', albeit a 'slippery, elusive, anonymous one'. Grimsby Street became a popular canvas for more established artists too and became a regular stop for organised walking tours of London's graffiti, the immediate area featuring in fashion photography shoots, film and television.

The premises of Barley Reproduction, furniture manufacturers, in one of the arches in Pedley Street

The railway bridge over Brick Lane, c 1976

Grimsby Street became a popular stop on walking tours of London due to the ever-changing displays of graffiti and contemporary art

The railways

arrive in Dalston

In the early 19th century, Dalston was a small village to the north of the city. It was concentrated around the junction of Balls Pond Road with Kingsland Road, a northwards continuation of Bishopsgate and Shoreditch High Street. Maps from the time show that Dalston was already starting to expand, as landowners and speculative house builders developed the areas to the south of Balls Pond Road and Dalston Lane. A regular grid of streets, with terraces of housing, was developed on the eastern side of Kingsland Road and, to the west, De Beauvoir Town was constructed by William Rhodes.

This speculative development, which began in the 1820s, was intended to consist of villas for the upper classes, laid out in a grid pattern with diagonal intersecting streets, but

Rhodes was hit by legal problems. Construction had to stop, and the prospective upper-class residents headed for the West End instead. The development was scaled down and building began again in the 1840s, with housing constructed for the emerging middle classes instead.

In 1850 the East & West India Docks & Birmingham Junction Railway (later renamed as the snappier 'North London Railway') arrived in Dalston. A station was built in Kingsland High Street, and in 1865 a branch from Dalston to a new terminus opened in the City at Broad Street. The new line cut through the back gardens of many of the houses on the eastern side of Kingsland Road, but created relatively few of the poverty-stricken backwaters that Charles Booth had seen in Shoreditch.

Several of the buildings that were recorded in Dalston as part of the East London Line Project date to this period of expansion in the late 19th and early 20th centuries, and were purpose-built as shops, some with offices and living accommodation on the upper floors. Dalston was now within easy commuting reach of the City and, along with further housing, Kingsland High Street developed as a shopping area. This character is reflected on Charles Booth's 1898 map of London poverty, which indicates that Dalston was populated largely by members of the middle classes, in contrast to the areas around the railway viaduct in Shoreditch to the south, which apparently lay at the heart of an area containing the poorest members of society.

Greenwood's map of London of 1827 shows how Dalston was a small village to the north of London, and was being developed as an attractive place for the upper classes to live

Booth's map of London poverty, showing how within a few decades London had expanded to swallow up Dalston

Kingsland High Street in the early 20th century

All change!

Dalston today

During the 20th century Dalston continued to see rapid change. The area became a centre for entertainment, with no fewer than four cinemas and a number of public houses shown on a map from 1916. Dalston Theatre, which was demolished in 2007, had opened as a circus in 1886, but was quickly converted to a variety theatre, and then a cinema in 1920. After the cinema closed in 1960, the building was put to a number of uses, including a car show room, and the Four Aces Nightclub, which played host to a number of famous acts, including Bob Marley and Stevie Wonder.

One of the buildings that was recorded for the East London Line Project was formerly Neuberg & Co's Cinematograph Theatre in Kingsland Road, which was partially rebuilt after the Second World War; a snooker club was opened on the first floor, and the ground floor was converted to a shop. The last occupants of the building were Oxfam, and in October 2007 the branch hosted a series of live gigs by the likes of Jarvis Cocker and Fatboy Slim, in aid of the charity's work, continuing a long tradition of live music in the area.

Some large areas of housing in Dalston were badly damaged by bombing during the Second World War, although the area around Kingsland Road and the High Street survived largely unscathed. The Metropolitan Borough of Hackney took the opportunity to clear large areas of 19th-century terraces and build social housing; as a consequence the grid of streets on the eastern side of the railway line was largely removed.

Dalston was in economic decline when the station at Dalston Junction, which provided a direct transport link with the City, closed in 1986, further exacerbating the area's problems. Attempts were made to regenerate the area and a shopping centre opened on the site of railway sidings on the eastern side of Kingsland High Street in the 1990s. Dalston has remained a vibrant place, with Ridley Road market and many independently owned shops lining Kingsland High Street serving a very diverse population.

The site of Neuberg & Co's Cinematograph Theatre in Kingsland Road

The King's Arms pub in Kingsland High Street

The interior of one of the shops in Kingsland High Street

67

What happens after the excavation?

Excavation may be the public face of archaeology, but equally important is the work carried out afterwards, in the office and laboratory. The analysis of the excavated layers and features, based on surveyed drawings, written records and photographs, is carried out in conjunction with the study of any available historical records, and the specialist analysis of finds (building materials, pottery and glass, metal, bone and wood objects) and environmental evidence (seeds and pollen, animal, bird and human bones, shells and insect remains) from the site, which can throw light on the dating and function of excavated features and buildings.

Pottery, for example, is categorised by fabric (type of clay and tempering material used), source (relation to known pottery production centres and their products), form (jug, bowl, plate etc) and function (tableware, cooking pots etc). Pottery is widely used as a major source of dating evidence for excavated site sequences; it can often be independently dated by reference to known dated examples. Human bone analysis, which will be carried out on the Roman and medieval burials found in the East London Line Project excavations, can tell us the age and sex of the individuals buried, and can provide information about general health as well as specific diseases and injuries.

When all the analyses are complete and drawn together, the resulting conclusions will be prepared for final publication, including monographs on the Shoreditch 'core' excavations and the railways' history. The finds and records will be stored in the Museum of London, and will be available by prior arrangement with the Museum's London Archaeological Archive and Research Centre (LAARC), 46 Eagle Wharf Road, London N1 7ED.

Part of an elaborate ?16th-century copper-alloy candle holder from a post-medieval rubbish pit on the Holywell Priory site

And finally . . .

In the final analysis, though there may be some surprises when the post-excavation work is completed, we can now describe the changing history of a section of Shoreditch from medieval Holywell Priory in the west to modern Pedley Street in the east, from Roman Ermine Street to the 21st-century East London line.

A glimpse of prehistoric occupation is seen in the stone tools found. The sparsely-occupied hinterland of Roman *Londinium* either side of Ermine Street was used for occasional burials. Gradual medieval development came with the foundation of Holywell Priory on one side of Shoreditch High Street, contrasting with the outskirts of the village of Shoreditch lining the other. East of this much of the area remained open fields. The growth of early post-medieval occupation, notably the earls of Rutland's Tudor mansion on the site of the priory, followed the Dissolution. The spread of the suburbs from the 17th century onwards encouraged large-scale quarrying of brickearth and brickmaking on the expanding periphery of new occupation, to the east of Shoreditch High Street. By the mid 18th century the character of the area had completely changed, and it was covered with suburban housing. In the early 19th century, the railway cut through the area, and developed in a complex sequence of expansions during the course of the century, notably those associated with Bishopsgate Goods Yard and access to Liverpool Street Station. The standing building records for railway structures along a much larger route, from Dalston in the north to Surrey Quays in the south, describe and illustrate the changing character of the railway from its 19th-century origins to modern uses of the railway arches, especially in the Shoreditch area.

These fieldwork results are clearly of considerable local significance, but are also of regional significance in showing the spread of urbanisation in London across what had originally been the City's hinterland. Information of national significance includes that from the medieval and Tudor Holywell Priory site and the early 19th-century railway structures.

An unusual post-medieval carved bone crucifixion, with a ?sun above, from the Bishopsgate Goods Yard site; probably a devotional aid

London Overground: the capital's new rail network

Artist's impression of Shoreditch High Street

In June 2010 when the East London line reopens to passenger services after major extension work, the line will become part of the London Overground network.

London Overground runs on the Richmond to Stratford, Clapham Junction to Willesden Junction, Gospel Oak to Barking and Watford Junction to Euston lines. When the East London line is connected to the Richmond to Stratford line at Highbury & Islington in 2011 and connected to Clapham Junction in 2012, London Overground services will form an orbital railway around London.

New step-free stations
The East London line has been extended north and will soon be calling at four, brand new, step-free stations at Shoreditch High Street, Hoxton, Haggerston and Dalston Junction. The East London line will run to West Croydon, Crystal Palace and New Cross in the south.

Brand new trains
The East London line will have brand new air-conditioned trains onto the Overground network that offers a high-frequency service similar to the London Underground.

Train benefits will include:

- more space – wider gangways to create more capacity

- greater security – clear sightlines for passengers and on-board CCTV

- faster boarding and alighting – wider doors and aisles to reduce waiting times

- improved accessibility – wheelchair ramps and dedicated wheelchair bays

- real-time information – on-board audio and visual announcements

- more pleasant journeys – air conditioning, wider seats and more handrails.

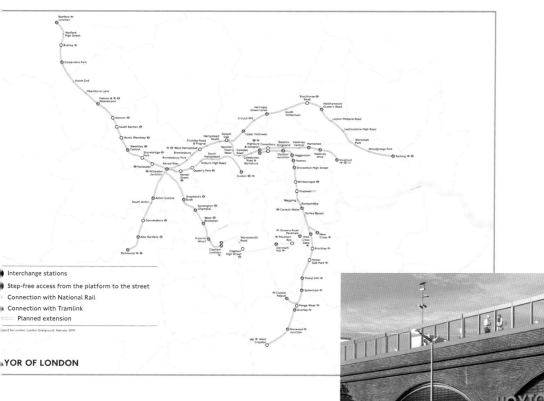

Interchange stations
Step-free access from the platform to the street
Connection with National Rail
Connection with Tramlink
Planned extension

Transport for London. London Overground. February 2009

*Artist's impression
of Hoxton station*

Creating London Overground

*Artist's impression
of a new East
London line train*

Transport for London OVERGROUND

Places to visit

The Building Exploratory
8 Orsman Road
Hackney
London N1 5QJ
Tel: 020 7729 2011
http://www.buildingexploratory.org.uk
Based in Hackney, East London, the Building Exploratory helps people to discover the secrets of their local area and gain a better understanding of the buildings and spaces that surround them

The Geffrye Museum
Kingsland Road
London E2 8EA
Tel: 020 7739 9893
http://www.geffrye-museum.org.uk
The collections of furniture, textiles, paintings and decorative arts are displayed in a series of period rooms from 1600 to the present day

London Transport Museum
Covent Garden Piazza
London WC2E 7BB
Tel: 020 7379 6344
http://www.ltmuseum.co.uk
A vital part of London's success was the transport system that developed alongside the capital in the 19th and 20th centuries – truly the lifeblood of this great city. The railway boom of the 1830s and 1840s saw routes to London created from every direction

Museum of London
London Wall
London EC2Y 5HN
Tel: 020 7001 9844
http://www.museumoflondon.org.uk
Discover prehistoric London, see how the city changed under Roman rule, and wonder at medieval London

Museum of London Docklands
West India Quay
Canary Wharf
London E14 4AL
Tel: 020 7001 9844
http://www.museumindocklands.org.uk
From Roman settlement to Docklands' regeneration, Museum of London Docklands reveals the long history of London as a port through stories of trade, migration and commerce

Sutton House
2 & 4 Homerton High Street
Hackney
London E9 6JQ
Tel: 020 8986 2264
http://www.nationaltrust.org.uk/main/w-suttonhouse
A Tudor house surviving in the heart of a thriving East London community, with authentic Tudor kitchen with objects to touch and smell

Further reading

Barron, C M, and Davies, M, 2007 The religious houses of London and Middlesex, London

Bull, M, 2007 Banksy, locations and tours: a collection of graffiti locations and photographs in London, London

Casella, E C, and Symonds, J, (eds) 2005 Industrial archaeology: future directions, New York

Gilchrist, R, 1994 Gender and material culture: the archaeology of religious women, London

Hawkins, C, 1990 The Great Eastern in town and country, Bedford

Hackney Society 1986 South Shoreditch, historical and industrial buildings, Hackney Society Report, London

Lichtenstein, R, 2007 On Brick Lane, London

Mander, D, 1996 More light, more power: an illustrated history of Shoreditch, Stroud

Penrose, S, 2007 Images of change: an archaeology of England's contemporary landscape, Swindon

Ross, C, and Clark, J, 2008 London: the illustrated history, London

Simmons, J, 2009 The Victorian railway, London

Survey of London, 1922 Survey of London: Vol 8, Shoreditch (ed J Bird), London

Vaughan, A, 2006 Brunel: an engineering biography, Hersham

Wolmar, C, 2008 Fire and steam: a new history of the railways in Britain, London